This

DIY-Investors 2019 Journal

Belongs to

_____

If found, please ring _____

Contents   Page

Past Performance of DIY-Investors' Portfolios

DIY-Investors Active 10 Portfolio Performance (Annual Records)

DIY-Investors : Active 10 Stock Portfolio					Portfolio (Cumulative % Change)
Year	ASX (% change)	ASX (Cumulative % change)	Active 10 Portfolio (% Change)	Annual Out-performance	Portfolio (Cumulative % Change)
2010	11.33	1.1133	18.73%	7.40	1.1873
2011	-6.69	1.0367	13.70%	20.39	1.3500
2012	8.24	1.1206	7.33%	-0.91	1.4490
2013	16.69	1.3076	30.42%	13.73	1.8898
2014	-2.13	1.2797	39.08%	41.21	2.6283
2015	-2.50	1.2477	47.33%	49.83	3.8723
2016	12.45	1.4030	46.69%	34.24	5.6803
2017	9.10	1.5307	36.72%	27.62	7.7661
2018					
	Average (to 31.12.2017) :		30.00%	24.19%	

Recent History of the All-Share Index (ASX)				
Year	ASX (at start)	ASX (at end)	Gain (loss)	ASX (% change)
2010	2,751.00	3,062.80	311.80	11.33
2011	3,062.80	2,857.90	-204.90	-6.69
2012	2,857.90	3,093.40	235.50	8.24
2013	3,093.40	3,609.60	516.20	16.69
2014	3,609.60	3,532.70	-76.90	-2.13
2015	3,532.70	3,444.26	-88.44	-2.50
2016	3,444.26	3,873.22	428.96	12.45
2017	3,873.22	4,225.61	352.39	9.10
2018	4,225.61			
			Average (to 31.12.2017) :	5.81%

You may wish to complete the table by adding the figures for 31st December 2018 (not available at time of printing)

Performance of DIY-Investors' 2018 Active 10 Portfolio

2018 Active 10 Stock Portfolio - compared to All-Share Index (ASX)

Index / Portfolio	31.12.2017	31st Jan	29th Feb	31st Mar	30th Apr	31st May	30th June	31st July	31st Aug	30th Sept	31st Oct	30th Nov	31st Dec
ASX	4225.61	4137.70	3981.60	3894.17	4127.68	4222.20	4202.30	4253.30	4106.14	4127.90	3904.23	3823.34	
ASX Change (%)	0.00	-2.08	-3.77	-2.20	6.00	2.29	1.81	0.74	-2.29	-2.95	-4.92	-7.38	
ASX Cumulative Change (%)	0.00	-2.08	-5.77	-7.84	-2.32	-0.08	-0.55	0.66	-2.83	-2.31	-7.61	-9.52	
Active 10 Portfolio (A10)													
A10 Value (£)	10000.00	10686.02	11953.73	10564.68	10333.19	11196.41	11047.30	10342.94	10804.29	11538.00	13021.80	12756.72	
A10 Change (%)	0.00	6.86	11.86	-11.62	-2.19	8.35	-1.33	-7.62	-2.20	11.55	20.52	10.56	
A10 Cumulative Change (%)	0.00	6.86	19.54	5.65	3.33	11.96	10.47	3.43	8.04	15.38	30.22	27.57	
A10 % relative to ASX	0.00	8.94	25.31	13.49	5.65	12.04	11.02	2.77	10.87	17.69	37.82	37.09	

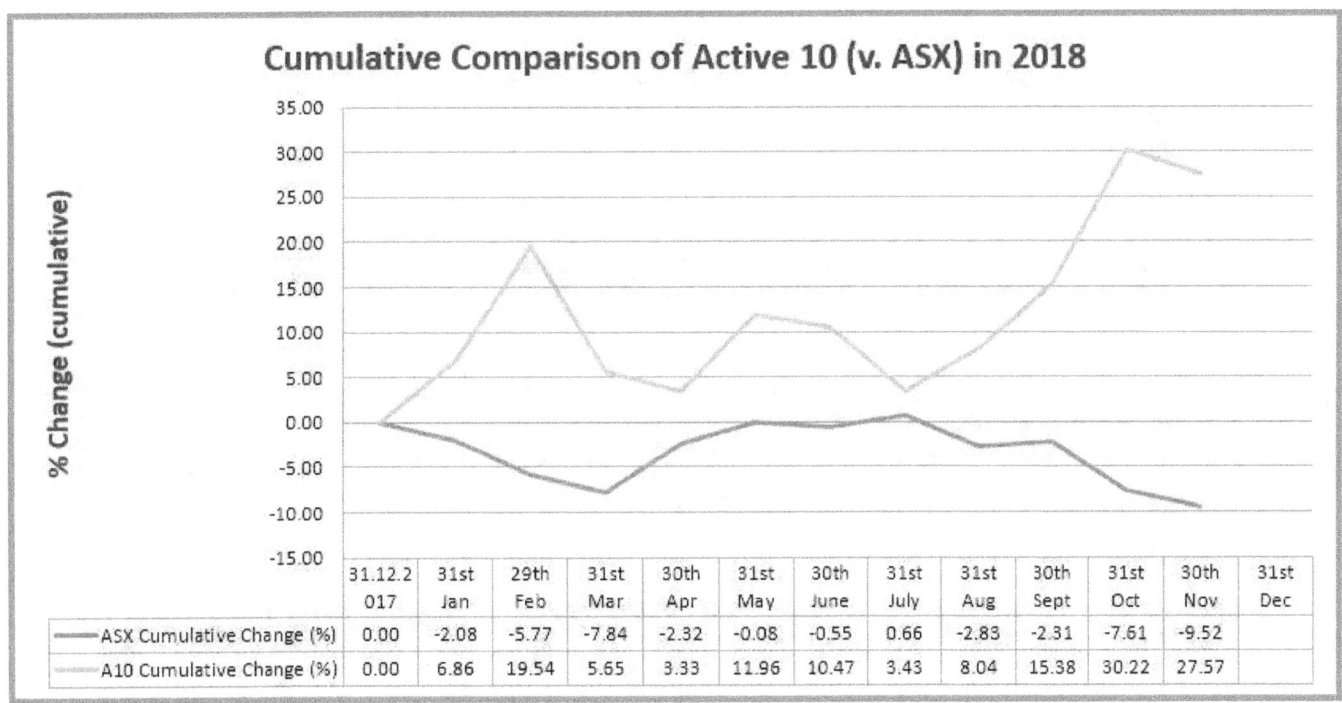

Cumulative Comparison of Active 10 (v. ASX) in 2018

	31.12.2017	31st Jan	29th Feb	31st Mar	30th Apr	31st May	30th June	31st July	31st Aug	30th Sept	31st Oct	30th Nov	31st Dec
ASX Cumulative Change (%)	0.00	-2.08	-5.77	-7.84	-2.32	-0.08	-0.55	0.66	-2.83	-2.31	-7.61	-9.52	
A10 Cumulative Change (%)	0.00	6.86	19.54	5.65	3.33	11.96	10.47	3.43	8.04	15.38	30.22	27.57	

You may wish to complete the table by adding the figures for 31st December 2018 (not available at time of printing)

DIY-Investors 2019 Calendar

January
S	M	T	W	T	F	S
		1	2	3	4	5
6	7	8	9	10	11	12
13	14	15	16	17	18	19
20	21	22	23	24	25	26
27	28	29	30	31		

February
S	M	T	W	T	F	S
					1	2
3	4	5	6	7	8	9
10	11	12	13	14	15	16
17	18	19	20	21	22	23
24	25	26	27	28		

March
S	M	T	W	T	F	S
					1	2
3	4	5	6	7	8	9
10	11	12	13	14	15	16
17	18	19	20	21	22	23
24	25	26	27	28	29	30
31						

April
S	M	T	W	T	F	S
	1	2	3	4	5	6
7	8	9	10	11	12	13
14	15	16	17	18	19	20
21	22	23	24	25	26	27
28	29	30				

May
S	M	T	W	T	F	S
			1	2	3	4
5	6	7	8	9	10	11
12	13	14	15	16	17	18
19	20	21	22	23	24	25
26	27	28	29	30	31	

June
S	M	T	W	T	F	S
						1
2	3	4	5	6	7	8
9	10	11	12	13	14	15
16	17	18	19	20	21	22
23	24	25	26	27	28	29
30						

July
S	M	T	W	T	F	S
	1	2	3	4	5	6
7	8	9	10	11	12	13
14	15	16	17	18	19	20
21	22	23	24	25	26	27
28	29	30	31			

August
S	M	T	W	T	F	S
				1	2	3
4	5	6	7	8	9	10
11	12	13	14	15	16	17
18	19	20	21	22	23	24
25	26	27	28	29	30	31

September
S	M	T	W	T	F	S
1	2	3	4	5	6	7
8	9	10	11	12	13	14
15	16	17	18	19	20	21
22	23	24	25	26	27	28
29	30					

October
S	M	T	W	T	F	S
		1	2	3	4	5
6	7	8	9	10	11	12
13	14	15	16	17	18	19
20	21	22	23	24	25	26
27	28	29	30	31		

November
S	M	T	W	T	F	S
					1	2
3	4	5	6	7	8	9
10	11	12	13	14	15	16
17	18	19	20	21	22	23
24	25	26	27	28	29	30

December
S	M	T	W	T	F	S
1	2	3	4	5	6	7
8	9	10	11	12	13	14
15	16	17	18	19	20	21
22	23	24	25	26	27	28
29	30	31				

Provisional Dates, for the DIY-Investors' Inner Circle Webinars are on the following Wednesdays:

Jan 9th, Feb 6th, Mar 6th, Apr 10th, May 8th, June 5th, July 10th, August 7th, Sept 11th. Oct 9th, Nov 6th & Dec 11th

www.diy-investors.com

INDEX

EPIC	Name						
		5					
EPIC	Name						

INDEX

EPIC	Name						
EPIC	Name						

INDEX

EPIC	Name						
EPIC	Name						

INDEX

EPIC	Name						
EPIC	Name						

INDEX

EPIC	Name						
EPIC	Name						

_____ : 2019 Active 10 Portfolio   *[This is your Portfolio to run alongside the DIY-Investors Active 10 Portfolio]*

Name (& Epic code)	Units	As at 31.12.2018 Ask Price	Value (£)	As at 31st March 2019 Bid Price	Value (£)	Change (YTD) (%)	As at 30th June 2019 Bid Price	Value (£)	Change (YTD) (%)	As at 30th September 2019 Bid Price	Value (£)	Change (YTD) (%)	As at 31st December 2019 Bid Price	Value (£)	Change (YTD) (%)
1															
2															
3															
4															
5															
6															
7															
8															
9															
10															
11															
12															
13															
14															
15															
16															
17															
18															

Cash (balancing figure to bring total to £10K) : £   Cash : £   Cash : £   Cash : £   Cash : £

Total (£): 10,000.00   Total (£): 0.00   Total (£): 0.00   Total (£): 0.00   Total (£): 0.00

	As at 31st March 2019	As at 30th June 2019	As at 30th September 2019	As at 31st December 2019
Overall Gain/Loss (£) :				
P'folio (cum) + / - (%) :				
ASX at end of month :				
Difference (points) :				
ASX (Cum %) +/-				
Portfolio (%) - v - ASX :				

ASX at start of 2019 : _____

10

DIY - Investors : 2019 Active 10 Portfolio

Name (& Epic code)	Units	As at 31.12.2018		As at 31st March 2019		Change (YTD)	As at 30th June 2019		Change (YTD)	As at 30th September 2019		Change (YTD)	As at 31st December 2019		Change (YTD)
		Ask Price	Value (£)	Bid Price	Value (£)	(%)	Bid Price	Value (£)	(%)	Bid Price	Value (£)	(%)	Bid Price	Value (£)	(%)
1															
2															
3															
4															
5															
6															
7															
8															
9															
10															
11															
12															
13															
14															
15															
16															
17															
18															

Cash (balancing figure to bring total to £10K) : £

| | Total (£): | 10,000.00 | | Cash : £ | Total (£): | 0.00 | | Cash : £ | Total (£): | 0.00 | | Cash : £ | Total (£): | 0.00 | | Cash : £ | Total (£): | 0.00 |

Overall Gain/Loss (£) :	Overall Gain/Loss (£) :	Overall Gain/Loss (£) :	Overall Gain/Loss (£) :
P'folio (cum) + / - (%) :	P'folio (cum) + / - (%) :	P'folio (cum) + / - (%) :	P'folio (cum) + / - (%) :
ASX at end of month :	ASX at end of month :	ASX at end of month :	ASX at end of month :
Difference (points) :	Difference (points) :	Difference (points) :	Difference (points) :
ASX (Cum %) +/-	ASX (Cum %) +/-	ASX (Cum %) +/-	ASX (Cum %) +/-
Portfolio (%) - v - ASX :	Portfolio (%) - v - ASX :	Portfolio (%) - v - ASX :	Portfolio (%) - v - ASX :

ASX at start of 2019 : _____

11

_____ : **2019 Passive 10 Portfolio**   [This is your Portfolio to compare against the DIY-investors Passive 10 Portfolio]

Name (& Epic code)	Units	As at 31.12.2018 Ask Price	Value (£)	As at 31st March 2019 Bid Price	Value (£)	Change (YTD) (%)	As at 30th June 2019 Bid Price	Value (£)	Change (YTD) (%)	As at 30th September 2019 Bid Price	Value (£)	Change (YTD) (%)	As at 31st December 2019 Bid Price	Value (£)	Change (YTD) (%)
1															
2															
3															
4															
5															
6															
7															
8															
9															
10															

Cash (balancing figure to bring total to £10K): £

Total (£):		10,000.00		Total (£):	0.00		Total (£):	0.00		Total (£):	0.00		Total (£):	0.00	

Cash : £   (31st March 2019)
Cash : £   (30th June 2019)
Cash : £   (30th September 2019)
Cash : £   (31st December 2019)

Overall Gain/Loss (£) :
P'folio (cum) + / - (%) :
ASX at end of month :
Difference (points) :
ASX (Cum %) +/-
Portfolio (%) - v - ASX :

Overall Gain/Loss (£) :
P'folio (cum) + / - (%) :
ASX at end of month :
Difference (points) :
ASX (Cum %) +/-
Portfolio (%) - v - ASX :

Overall Gain/Loss (£) :
P'folio (cum) + / - (%) :
ASX at end of month :
Difference (points) :
ASX (Cum %) +/-
Portfolio (%) - v - ASX :

Overall Gain/Loss (£) :
P'folio (cum) + / - (%) :
ASX at end of month :
Difference (points) :
ASX (Cum %) +/-
Portfolio (%) - v - ASX :

ASX at start of 2019 : _____

12

DIY-Investors : 2019 Passive 10 Portfolio

Name (& Epic code)	Units	As at 31.12.2018 Ask Price	Value (£)	As at 31st March 2019 Bid Price	Value (£)	Change (YTD) (%)	As at 30th June 2019 Bid Price	Value (£)	Change (YTD) (%)	As at 30th September 2019 Bid Price	Value (£)	Change (YTD) (%)	As at 31st December 2019 Bid Price	Value (£)	Change (YTD) (%)
1															
2															
3															
4															
5															
6															
7															
8															
9															
10															
Cash (balancing figure to bring total to £10K): £				Cash : £			Cash : £			Cash : £			Cash : £		
Total (£):	10,000.00			Total (£):	0.00		Total (£):	0.00		Total (£):	0.00		Total (£):	0.00	

Overall Gain/Loss (£) :

P'folio (cum) + / - (%) :

ASX at end of month :

Difference (points) :

ASX (Cum %) +/-

Portfolio (%) - v - ASX :

ASX at start of 2019 : _____

13

Webinar Notes   (Inner Circle Webinar _____ 2019)

Webinar Notes   (Inner Circle Webinar _____ 2019)

Webinar Notes   (Inner Circle Webinar _____ 2019)

Webinar Notes   (Inner Circle Webinar _____ 2019)

Webinar Notes   (Inner Circle Webinar _____ 2019)

Webinar Notes   (Inner Circle Webinar _____ 2019)

Webinar Notes   (Inner Circle Webinar _____ 2019)

Webinar Notes   (Inner Circle Webinar _____ 2019)

Webinar Notes   (Inner Circle Webinar _____ 2019)

Webinar Notes   (Inner Circle Webinar _____ 2019)

Webinar Notes   (Inner Circle Webinar _____ 2019)

Webinar Notes   (Inner Circle Webinar _____ 2019)

Webinar Notes   (Inner Circle Webinar _____ 2019)

Webinar Notes   (Inner Circle Webinar _____ 2019)

NOTES

NOTES

NOTES

NOTES

NOTES

NOTES

NOTES

NOTES

NOTES

NOTES

NOTES

NOTES

NOTES

NOTES

NOTES

NOTES

NOTES

NOTES

NOTES

NOTES

NOTES

NOTES

NOTES

NOTES

NOTES

52

NOTES

NOTES

NOTES

NOTES

NOTES

NOTES

NOTES

NOTES

NOTES

NOTES

NOTES

NOTES

NOTES

NOTES

NOTES

NOTES

NOTES

NOTES

NOTES

NOTES

NOTES

NOTES

NOTES

NOTES

NOTES

NOTES

NOTES

NOTES

NOTES

NOTES

NOTES

NOTES

NOTES

NOTES

NOTES

NOTES

NOTES

NOTES

NOTES

NOTES

NOTES

NOTES

NOTES

NOTES

NOTES

NOTES

NOTES

NOTES

NOTES

NOTES

NOTES

NOTES

NOTES

NOTES

NOTES

NOTES

NOTES

NOTES

NOTES

NOTES

NOTES

NOTES

NOTES

NOTES

NOTES

NOTES

NOTES

NOTES

NOTES

NOTES

NOTES

Thank You for purchasing a copy of the

2019 DIY-Investors Journal

As a special "Thank You", we are pleased to provide you with the following bonuses:

- Free Access to the next "Inner Circle Webinar" (worth more than the cost of this journal!)
- A complimentary pdf "Guide to Using Your DIY-Investors Journal"

To find out how to access these bonuses, visit the following page on the DIY-Investors website:

http://diy-investors.com/2019-diy-jnoffer/

When prompted, enter the password **DIYJ2019**

About the Author

Mick Pavey is an active private investor, Company Director, business owner and Chartered Surveyor. He lives in Shropshire and splits his time between his investing activities, helping small businesses and taking part in his hobbies (Art, Dancing & Photography).

Mick is a keen investor, specialising in combining fundamental and technical analysis. He is a founder member of http://diy-investors.com – a community of like-minded, independent investors that share views and research.

His book "Picking Winning Shares" can be found on Amazon at : http://amzn.to/2kiH2bA

He also writes a blog which can be found at:
 http://diy-investors.blogspot.com

and… occasionally he tweets at:
http://twitter.com/DIYinvestors

About the Publisher

Ditty Box Publishing

Ditty Box Publishing is located in the Shropshire Hills.

It supports authors, artists, crafters & entrepreneurs, by providing publishing & printing services to the community.

Ditty Box Publishing is a division of Ditty Box Ltd, a company registered in England (No. 4602831).

Contact Details

Website: dittyboxpublishing.com

E-Mail: admin@dittyboxpublishing.com

www.ingramcontent.com/pod-product-compliance
Lightning Source LLC
Chambersburg PA
CBHW080943170626
46813CB00008B/3121